Will You Eat a Tree Today?

Will You Eat a Tree Today?

Poems for Kids and Other Strange Beings

by

Adam Stockman

© 2025 Adam Stockman. All rights reserved.
This material may not be reproduced in any form, published,
reprinted, recorded, performed, broadcast,
rewritten or redistributed without
the explicit permission of Adam Stockman.
All such actions are strictly prohibited by law.

Cover image by Adam Stockman
Other images by Adam Stockman
Author photo by Adam Stockman

ISBN: 978-1-63980-836-6

Kelsay Books
502 South 1040 East, A-119
American Fork, Utah 84003
Kelsaybooks.com

Upon this page
I'd like to thank
Whomever is reading
So, fill in the blank: _____

Acknowledgments

This book would not be here without the support of my family, Courtney and Kinnell.

And, of course, Michelle who was my first and most enthusiastic fan (and thank you, Michelle, for coloring the cover of this book).

Contents

The Snake	13
News Flash!	14
The Dandelion Wish	15
Giraffe Laughter	16
Please Leaf	17
Literally . . .	18
High-Level Math	19
This Delicious Universe	20
Rabbit, Squirrel, Rat	21
The Ostrich (of Sorts)	23
Dinosaur Ghosts	24
Have You Seen My . . . ?	26
How to Write!!!!	27
Emma Jo's Nose	30
A Question About Umbrellas	31
Witch Baby	33
Dapple Duty	36
True Colors	37
Here Comes the (Sun?)	39
They Stink!	40
Impossible Asks, Impossible Acts	41
Will You Eat a Tree Today?	44
Corn-on-the-Corn-on-the . . .	46
An Ode to a Toad	48
Winning Poem	49
Put It Down	50
Ode to a Skink	51
Listen to Your Librarian!	53
Coloring	56
A Poem of the Heart	57
Planet of the Ants	58

A Lot of a Lots	59
Mrs. Constrictor	60
Roar!	61
Summer's End	62
A Quest for Questions	63
Solar Camels	64
The Song of Autumn	65
Dinosaur Shopping Mall	66
Everything Should Have Pockets	68
Time to Choose	70
Friend Window	71
Where Did It Go My Tomato?	74
Can You Top That?	75
How Do You See the Mimliodee?	76
The Kid in the Bathroom Mirror	78
More Homework	80
Who Loves the Rain?	81
Semantic Antics	83
Pandas	83
The End of the Book	85

The Snake

A funny fellow is the snake,
I'll tell you what I mean:
He has a head, he has a tail,
But nothing in between.

News Flash!

If you're asking for my daily news,
I woke up this morning and wore the wrong shoes.
If you ask my shoes, they'll disagree,
They'll tell you they woke up and wore the wrong me.

The Dandelion Wish

On dandelion fluff I blew me a wish,
The seeds rose like hope through the breezes.
I wished for friendship, I wished for peace,
All I got was the loudest of sneezes.

Giraffe Laughter

If you tell a joke to a giraffe,
Don't be upset if it doesn't laugh.
The joke has to first meet the brain and go south,
Down to the belly then back through the mouth.
With that long, long neck it's a heck of a ways . . .
That laugh may take a couple of days.

Young Teesha McQuaid, she wanted to hear it,
So, she found a giraffe and crept very near it.
She told it the joke about the chicken and the road,
Then she camped out for ninety-nine days in a row.
The giraffe opened wide as if laughter might roar . . .
Instead, it said, "That one I've heard before."

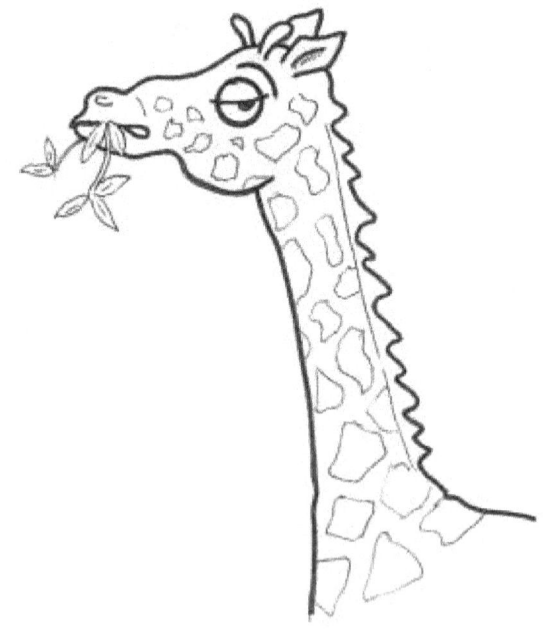

Please Leaf

I had a leaf. I named him Steve.
I said to him, "It's time to leave."
He looked at me and said, "Good grief!
The proper phrase is 'time to leaf.'"

Literally . . .

Yes, I punched my cup of fruit punch,
It seemed like the thing to do.
And then I squashed my summer squash.
Well, honestly, wouldn't you?
I chipped away at a potato chip,
Now it is half its size.
And I beat my plate of beets last night
Much to my mom's surprise.
And I had two friends, Rob and Pat,
But they stopped coming over. Now, why is that?

High-Level Math

There are so many numbers, an infinite sprawl,
Soon we will run out of names for them all.
Beyond quadrillion, as numbers keep mounting
We'll have to use words not intended for counting.
We'll reach a vast number called "table" and then,
We'll count up to "butterscotch," "bongo," and "hen."
When we've used up the words from our thick dictionary,
We'll have to invent ones like "blimble" and "klary."
I know it sounds crazy, a little absurd,
But limitless numbers need limitless words!
So, that's my excuse to you, Mrs. McGrath,
It wasn't a swear word . . .
Just high-level math.

This Delicious Universe

If the moon is cheese, then what is the sun?
An egg over-easy? A cinnamon bun?
What is Saturn? What are the stars?
Is the Milky Way made out of Milky Way bars?
Venus is swirling in pineapple juices,
Mercury's plainly been molded from mousses.
Mars is a big chunk of Turkish delight,
And Jupiter looks like a gobstopper, right?
This is the reason I'm going to space,
Not for the chance to be first in a race,
Not for adventure or deeds of great valor,
Or the chance to tap-dance through a meteor shower,
Not for the fame (I'm not that ambitious),
But just 'cause our universe looks so delicious!

Rabbit, Squirrel, Rat

I made up a game, it's easy to play:
Rabbit, squirrel, rat.
It's a fun thing to do at the start of the day:
Rabbit, squirrel, rat.
Out from behind a bush or a tree,
A small fuzzy thing will emerge-hard to see.
There are one of three things it will turn out to be:
Rabbit, squirrel, or rat.
If the miniature mystery creature in question,
Is judged to be rabbit on closer inspection,
Congratulations! A point you've earned!
If it's a squirrel you lose a turn.
If it's a rat . . . Game over! Burn!

Early last week I was playing my game:
Rabbit, squirrel, rat.
Some rabbits came out seeming ever so tame.
I counted them up. Ten! What a score!
I fed them some chocolate. Out came some more!
They followed me home to my own front door.
I adopted them all, those fine furry dudes.
They slept in my bed; they nibbled my foods.
On their wee bunny heads, I gave them all pats.
Oh, they were spoiled, those cute bunny brats!
I invited my brother to see them in hats.
He said, "Those aren't bunnies, you know, they are . . ."

The Ostrich (of Sorts)

The ostrich has a neck that's long,
Its wings are mighty, thick, and strong
(I mean they don't have any strength
Despite their thickness, heft, and length).
An ostrich can fly to the tops of trees
(Ones that grow to below your knees).
A few ostrich species can fly to the moon
(By "the moon" I mean as high as a prune).
So let us recap (and you can cite this):
The ostrich can fly (I mean it is flightless).

Dinosaur Ghosts

Some say the dinosaurs are all extinct,
But they're not as gone as you might think.
I hate to say it, you may not want it,
But the whole wide world might be dinosaur haunted!
Ghosts of the dinosaurs who came before us,
T-rex, Iguanodon and Ankylosaurus,
Walking around, beside and on top of us.
You might glimpse a galloping, ghostly Diplodocus!
Or maybe you'll hear some dinosaur moans:
"Give us back our dinosaur bones!
Bring them out! We want to see 'em!
Rescue our bones from the history museum!"
Don't be afraid, they're as fragile as paper,
They're really nothing but dinosaur vapor.
If you were attacked by a ghostly T-Rex,
He'd charge right through you, looking perplexed.

Will they wander forever as ghosts? That's sad.
But come to think of it, it might not be bad.
There'd be plenty of other spirits to see,
Other ghosts to keep them company.
They'd probably give dinosaur rides to Abe Lincoln
And Harriet Tubman, that's what I'm thinkin'.
And Joan of Arc would opt to teach tricks
To each and every Archaeopteryx.
So, maybe the world isn't haunted at all,
Maybe these ghosts are all having a ball!
It's less a spook-fest and more of a lark,
A phantasmagorical Jurassic Park.

Have You Seen My . . . ?

Secret hideouts are hidden,
They're not supposed to be found.
Sometimes they're up in a tree,
Sometimes they're deep underground.
There's usually a secret entrance
Hidden by bookshelves or rocks,
And a door which can only be opened
By pressing a statue or clock.
Did you know that I have a hideout?
It's under a nearby tree.
I hid it where no one can find it,
And I have the only key.
Why am I telling you this?
The fact is I need your help.
I hid my hideout so secretly
That I can't even find it myself.

How to Write!!!!

Hear ye! Hear ye! Gather round!
Listen to this incredible sound!
I'm teaching you lessons that won't disappoint!
It's how to use exclamation points!
For when you use this punctuation,
Your speech will cause a tremendous sensation!
It doesn't matter what you're writing,
An exclamation point will make it exciting!
For instance, behold! I'll write the word "Donut!"
Kinda looks more impressive now, don't it!
It's like you possess a magic wand
And whatever word you wave it upon
Becomes important! But why just one?
Two exclamation points is much more fun!!
Your readers need their attention grabbed!!
Your readers need their eyeballs stabbed!!

How else will they know your story is good?
With two exclamation points it's understood!!
Which is why you should take this advice from me:

INSTEAD OF TWO, YOU SHOULD MAKE IT THREE!!!
THREE EXCLAMATION POINTS!!! HOW EXCITING!!!
NO ONE ON EARTH WILL IGNORE YOUR WRITING!!!
AND I BET I CAUGHT YOU BY SURPRISE
WHEN YOU SAW EACH SENTENCE CAPITALIZED!!!
SURELY, WE CAN'T GO ANY FARTHER!!!
YES, WE CAN!!!! WITH TEXT THAT'S LARGER!!!!
TEXT GIGANTIC!!!! MORE!!!! MORE!!!! MORE!!!!
EXCLAMATIONS POINTS ARE NOW AT FOUR!!!!
THIS IS THE MOST EXCITING AND—

Ladies and gentlemen, please remain seated,
It's possible our lecturer became overheated.
She's had some sort of a fainting spasm,
Likely from too much enthusiasm.
It's true. I'm sorry. She really did.
The lecture is over now . . . period.

Emma Jo's Nose

There lived a girl named Emma Jo who craved a great adventure.
She longed to chase her dreams. Alas, her nose would never let her.
For every time poor Emma thought she'd jump or run with ease,
Emma's nose would fire off the most gigantical sneeze.
She tried to build a birthday cake upon a golden platter,
But then . . . achoo! Poor Emma Jo ker-sneezed into the batter.
She tried to climb a mountain in the windy days of Autumn,
But whoops! Achoo! Her sneezes made her tumble to the bottom.
She ran for classroom president. Alas, she was defeated.
For Emma's nose would always run more heavily than she did.
Her doctor sat her down and said, "Now listen, Emma Jo,
I ran some tests and here's some things I think you ought to know.
You're sensitive to eggplants, averse to lima beans,
Allergic to geraniums and also collard greens.
Stay away from chestnut trees, oaks and western yews,
Posies, roses, dandelions, berries, petting zoos.
Dog and cat and hamster hair will cause your eyes to swell,
Rabbit fur and llama feet and turtle toes as well.

The point I'm trying hard to make, my dear, for what it's worth,
Is frankly you're allergic to all living things on earth.
I have some medication here." Emma shook her head.
She went directly home and drew some grand designs instead.
For seven months, through sneezes huge, her work went on and on
Until, at last, a rocket towered high on Emma's lawn.
'Twas on a sunny Saturday, the seventeenth of June,
When Emma flew her rocket to the dark side of the moon.
And there she lives contentedly, nose no longer flowing,
Basking in a lunar land where nothing's ever growing.
Sure, it's cold, and often Emma's underwear will freeze,
But that's a price she's glad to pay to live without a sneeze.

A Question About Umbrellas

Do umbrellas work from afar?
Because I left mine in the car.

Witch Baby

My mom and dad came home last week with my newborn baby
 sister.
At first, she seemed all cute, you know, we cuddled her and kissed
 her.
But then an evil change occurred like someone flipped a switch.
I saw at last, from the spells she cast, my sister was a witch.

With her ga-ga goo-goo voodoo she turned dad into a zombie.
Late one night, I heard some creepy footsteps in the hallway.
To the kitchen I snuck, and there was dad, eyes staring blankly
 ahead.
His face looked etched, his arms outstretched, seemingly half-
 dead.

"Dad?" I said. He looked at me as if he hardly knew me.
"Bawble blah," he mumbled with his lips and chin all drooly.
He smelled like toads, his skin had scales, his voice held hints of doom.
I screamed in fright at the pitiful sight, and raced back to my room.

A change came over mom as well, she used to be quite neat,
Polished and in-fashion from her head down to her feet.
But one day I woke up to see she'd put her shirt on backwards.
Her hair was spiked and snarled as if she'd walked through six disasters.

"Out of the way," she barked at me with a deep and throaty growl.
She nearly bit my head off when I lost the baby's towel.
So, when the full moon rose last night, I hid inside the den
'Cause mom was now a werewolf, right? The witch had struck again.

I was sad to lose my parents but that's not what hurt the most,
The meanest spell my sister cast had turned me to a ghost.
Yes, I was invisible, people saw right through me.
I haunted my own hallways making noises grim and gloomy.

Finally, I had had enough, someone had to stop her.
Maybe I could mail her to a family who'd adopt her.
I marched into the nursery. "Listen up you witch!
I'm here to blow your dark and evil purposes to bits."

She reached to me with tiny arms, smiling at me above her . . .
Too late! She cast another spell. My sister made me love her.

Dapple Duty

The sun falls short on dappling. That is my belief.
Sure, it dapples quite a bit-the grass, the pond, the leaf.
But I would dapple so much more if I had dapple-duty.
I'd be the dapple-captain, yes, and spread the dapple beauty.

I'd start with my umbrella. I'd dapple that thing good.
The dappliest umbrella in the whole dang neighborhood.
I'd dapple it so heavily the rain would not come near,
Thinking it sun-dappled it would shrink away in fear.

I'd dapple all my windows, the doorknobs and the lattice,
I'd dapple my chinchilla then I'd dapple my aunt Gladys.
I'd point to every object in the house and holler, "Dapple!
Dapple this! And dapple that! Dapple that crabapple!"

I'd build a dappling catapult and launch my dapple-splats!
I'd dapple-splat my roof and then I'd dapple-splat my cats.
My house would be so dappled you'd prob'ly get upset.
Because you'd think the sun had opted to come live with me, I bet.

But I would not slow down, oh no! I couldn't slow my pace,
Not while dapple-lacking people lived in dapple-absent space!
I'd detonate a dapple-doozy nuclear device!
And turn the whole wide world into a dappled paradise!

Folks would gaze in wonder (and a few would prob'ly faint),
They'd think the gods themselves had gone and spilled a bunch of paint.
And then the world would dwell inside a dapple-dizzy vision,
There'd be no war or scarcity, no schisms or divisions.

And when my dapple-duty had been done, I'd surely rest.
Knowing that I'd dared to bring to life a dapple-fest.
I'd lay on dappled pillows as the dappled moonlight beamed,
And drift away contentedly in dapple-happy dreams.

True Colors

Those shades of beige,
Those fades of blue,
Those lines in the sky of a purplish hue.
That black, that gold, that stain of gray,
Brushed across clouds on this storm-stirred day.
I've looked in my crayon box,
Gone through my markers,
Combed through my paints from the lighters to darkers.
None of the colors I saw in the air
Can be found in my art supplies any-old-where!
Perhaps they weren't meant for gross replication
But only as soul-stirring, rich inspiration.
By flirting and teasing, remaining apart,
Those colors create in us longing and
 . . . art.

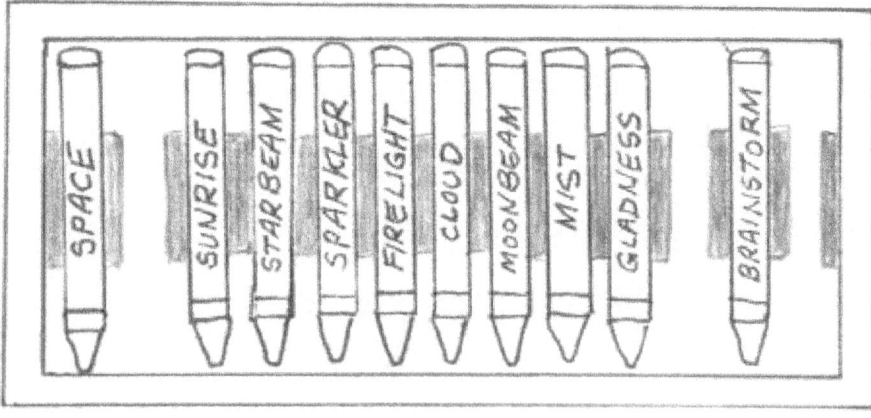

Here Comes the (Sun?)

Once, eons and eons ago,
(It was only a couple of weeks or so!)
An orb was up in the sky they say.
(You could see it yourself almost every day!)
It was yellow with purplish polka dots.
(The first part is right, the second is not!)
It sent its warmth to the good boys and girls.
(It warmed up everyone! The entire world!)
People called it "the Cinnamon Bun"
(No, you fool, it's called the sun!)
Is it an old wives tale? A myth?
(Seriously, dude? It really exists!)
Did it fly away? Did it fail? Did it fall?
(It's only some cloudy weather is all.)
I wish it would return; I do.
(Well, there I'd have to agree with you.)

They Stink!

Here come the stink bugs! They're everywhere!
(I think there's a stink bug asleep in your hair!)
There's one on the sofa, one in the sink!
Two on the mantle, and three in your drink!
What do they want? What do they need?
Are they here to explore? Or here to feed?
Maybe they've come as odor inspectors,
Or spies, or thieves, or stink collectors!
They find new scents and snatch them up,
Filling an extra-large "Smell-A-Fill" cup.
Then to a top-secret lab they take flight
Where stink bug scientists work through the night,
Mixing, combining, testing new scents.
What sort of smell do you think they'll invent?
It might be an odor so sprinkled with stink
That the world will surrender to them (they think).
Of that kind of theory, I'm a little unsure,
It's my belief that they're just insecure.

They come to our homes through front door and back
And land in our spaces to see how we'll react.
So, if a stink bug alights on your lap,
Greet it with "Hi" or "I love you" perhaps.
Tell them they're worthy of appreciation.
Tell them how lovely their marmoration.
And they'll leave you feeling so tickled and pleased,
Their self-esteem will be greatly increased.
If this love so fills them as you show them the door,
The hope is they won't need to come back for more.

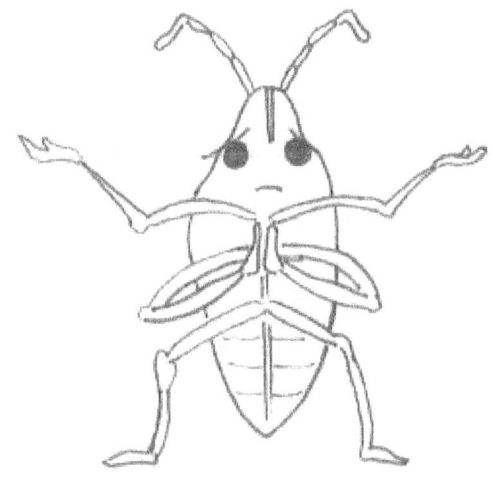

Impossible Asks, Impossible Acts

I hope someday
You run far away with a spoon.

I pray you sing
With a cow as it springs o'er the moon.

And please go and talk
With the jabberwock at length.

And wrestle with
A hippogryph if you feel have the strength.

All of these tasks
Are impossible asks you might sigh.

"Well, yes," I'd reply.
"That's the reason why you should try."

The weird and the strange
Can rearrange your view,

And lead you to say
That imaginative things may be true.

You might now lack this
Skill, but practice and sing

Til you're up in the sky
On a butterfly with dragon's wings.

And when you've decided
To truly run wild and free,

And you're up on the moon,
Say hello to the spoon for me.

Will You Eat a Tree Today?

Flimmles look a lot like us,
They go to school; they ride the bus.
Yet when they speak, you'll soon agree
They're not at all like you or me.
On planet Flimm "hello" is "hook,"
"Eat" means "read," and "tree" means "book."
So, if you hear somebody say,
"Hook, will you eat a tree today?"
They're probably not a her or him
But an alien from planet Flimm.
Follow closely, pay attention,
Here's another Flimmle lesson:
"Cat" means "swim" and "shirt" means "time,"
"Tree" means "when" and "night" means "slime."
How would you ask on planet Flimm,
When will it be time to swim?
If the answer you turned in after that
Was "Tree will it be shirt to cat?"

You got it right! You're not too slow,
You're learning Flimmle like a pro!
Here's a final lesson for now.
(Flimmle is easy, isn't it now!)
"Bug" means "eat," "hair" means "invade,"
"Leaf" means "Earth," "apple" means "glade,"
"Chair" means "humans," "spot" means "take,"
"Hammer" means "over," "Bob" means "lake."
If someone says, "It's shirt to hair,
Let's spot-hammer leaf and bug the chairs."
If you did well on your Flimmle exam,
Then you should know it's time to scram!

Corn-on-the-Corn-on-the . . .

I'm having some corn-on-the-cob for dinner,
Corn-on-the-cob is a sure-fire winner.
Then corn-on-the-cob will be coming right back
For dessert, I think, and a midnight snack.
Corn-on-the-cob for breakfast and lunch,
Corn-on-the-cob for an in-between munch.
But why must it always be corn-on-the-cob?
Why can't we give the corn some other job?
Like corn-on-the-chimney, corn-on-the-cat,
Corn-on-the-skyscraper, corn-on-the-hat?
Corn-on-the-corner, corn-in-a-nest,
Corn-on-my-taste-buds is what I like best.
Corn-on-my-teeth, corn-in-my-belly,
Corn-out-my-butt (which is corn rather smelly).
Corn-in-the-compost turning to soil,
Then corn sprouting up again ready to boil.
But I bet you can guess where the corn's most ingrained,
Because as you can see, I have corn-on-the-brain.

An Ode to a Toad

If you chance upon a garden toad,
I must report a rumor:
Some people say he hates a joke
And has no sense of humor.

He loathes a pun especially,
Like, "Hey, your car was toad!"
Or "How's your three-toad sloth today?"
And of course, "I toad you so."

He'll barely move a muscle,
His frown will be robust,
His bulging eyes will stare at you
With loathing and disgust.

Then again, on the other hand,
It's only fair to say,
Now that I seriously think about it . . .
Toads always look that way.

Winning Poem

A poetry contest seems wrong somehow,
In fact, just a little absurd.
Like trying to judge the best morning song
Among various sweet-singing birds.
It's a contradiction I think you'll agree
Because we all have a song to sing.
And to say one is prettier, or better or worse
Is to miss the whole point of the thing.

Put It Down

Out of the corner of my wandering eye
A message appeared on my phone,
Which sparked some pleasure and a happy sigh,
And I thought, *I am not alone.*

Someone loves me, someone cares,
Someone craves my attention,
But the very next instant I saw what it was:
An automated marketing message.

My mood went sour, I quickly despaired;
Would nobody text me or call?
I turned to the window and quietly stared,
Perhaps no one loved me at all.

In that silent, sad and pitying space
The sun angled down through the trees.
I felt it buttering my toasted face;
The sun was messaging me.

And gravity too, it said, "Here you go,
What a place to be held in today."
The leaves were waving and saying, "Hello."
The grass shouted, "Come out and play!"

I saw all the calls that went unheard-
Though they weren't coming through on my phone-
From the pebbles, the clouds, the ants, and the birds,
And they said: You are not alone.

Ode to a Skink

This is a verse about the blue tongued skink,
'Cause there ain't many written about it, I think.
Which to me is a shame 'cause its tongue is all blue.
A thing like that deserves a poem or two.
They write about buffalos, beavers, and cougars,
But the skink don't exactly inspire an oeuvre.
It's docile, gentle, and easily tamed,
So, it's not a creature that's often blamed
For startin' adventures or makin' a mess.
It just sits around and eats insects, I guess.
But I'd write an ode to the skink, wouldn't you?
'Cause dang! Look it up! Its tongue is all blue!

Listen to Your Librarian!

Fiona stood on the diving board, about to plunge on in.
She felt a breeze blow through her hair, the sun was on her skin.
She'd waited tensely through winter and spring to stand upon this board,
But her feet were frozen, she couldn't move! Then a voice behind her roared,
"There are twenty-eight kids in line back here! Why the sudden stall?
Are you afraid?" Fiona replied, "No, that's not it at all.

A book, a book, I need a good book! I have to be reading this summer!
Without a good plot, well, what have I got? My vacation will be a big bummer.
A book about lizards? A book about trucks? A book about mystical elves?
There are so many out there, I need to go quickly and search through the library shelves.
I have to be holding one now in my hands, it has to be researched and read!
A book! A book! I must have a book! Is what my librarian said."

Jacob sat in a roller coaster ready to go to the top.
He was buckled in and itching to go when he suddenly shouted "Stop!"
A man rushed over and said, "What's wrong? Are you scared to follow through?"
"No," said Jacob. "I'm sure this is great, but there's something else I must do.

A book, a book, I need a good book! I have to be reading this summer!
Without a good tale, I may as well bail. My vacation will be a big bummer.
A book about cooking? A book about snakes? A book about following tracks?
There are so many out there, I need to go quickly and search through the library stacks.
I have to be holding one now in my hands, it has to be researched and read!
A book! A book! I must have a book! Is what my librarian said."

And what about you? What are your plans? Some whitewater rafting in Maine?
Camping in Utah? Swimming? Surfing? A tour of cathedrals in Spain?

Whatever it is I hope there's a moment when all of a sudden you freeze,
Your eyes go wide, your hair stands up, you're helplessly weak in the knees.
And when someone asks you, "Hey, what's wrong? Dude, are you okay?"
You'll turn your head like a horror-film zombie and this is what you'll say:

"A book, a book, I need a good book! I have to be reading this summer!
Without a good fable, we might as well table vacation! A horrible bummer!
A book about dragons? A book about dancing? A book about candy bar wars?
There are so many out there, I need to go quickly and search through my local bookstores.
I have to be holding one now in my hands, it has to be researched and read!
A book! A book! I must have a book! Is what my librarian said."

Coloring

You can't make colors go away
By coloring. What a thing to say!
It's a paradox, a contradiction,
Illogical, an utter fiction.
But coloring brings me joy, okay?
Which is why I find I'm forced to say:
I'm coloring my blues away.

A Poem of the Heart

The way to make a work of art
Is to fill every sentence with "of the heart."
For instance, the tree of the heart is growing.
The wind of the heart is constantly blowing.
The math of the heart is not that hard.
The game of the heart is played in the yard.
The mashed potatoes of the heart are delicious.
The pit bull of the heart is vicious.
That toy I placed in my shopping cart
Is a Lego action figure of the heart.
You might think this poem is only for fools,
But I don't make up the poetry rules.
This poem, too, is a work of art,
As is all of the poetry of the heart.

Planet of the Ants

Scratch the surface of your average lawn,
Pull up any old plants,
Lift a log or a rock anywhere
And you're bound to find some ants.
That's why I'm certain the earth isn't made
Of magma or iron ore,
No, it's a vast ball of wriggling ants
Making up its core.

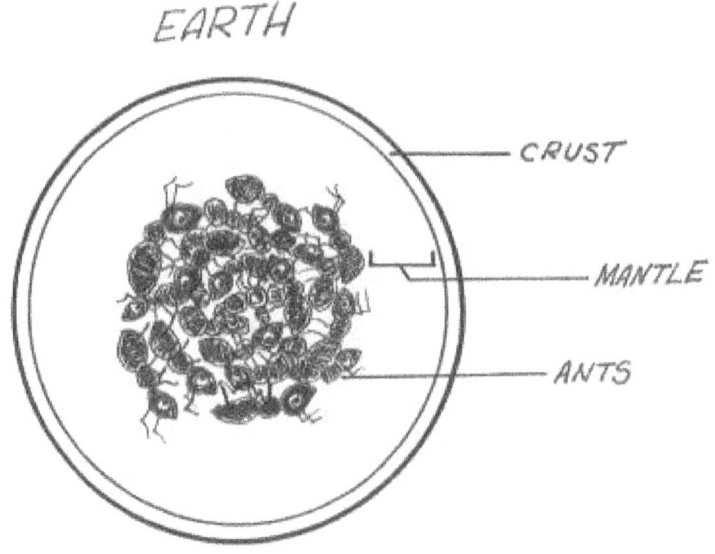

A Lot of a Lots

The ocelot likes sauce a lot,
It loves its sauce an awful lot.
Red sauce must be hot (a lot),
Green is made from moss (a lot),
But after eating sauce a lot,
The ocelot must floss a lot,
But sauce and floss, they cost a lot.
So, the ocelot is cross a lot.

Mrs. Constrictor

Hello! I'm a boa (Mrs. Constrictor).
My, you possess such an elegant figure.
I'm a boa from Goa. How strange we should meet.
I can tell we'll be friends. Ooh, what a treat!
You're so cute and cuddly! Please sit with me.
I could hug you to death! (Quite literally.)
Did you speak, my dear? I can't quite follow.
It might be because . . . you're so hard to swallow.

Roar!

Lions like to roar,
So does the dinosaur.
Crowds roar too, they say
When a player makes
A brilliant play.
Oceans roar along the shore,
And in a shell a little more.
Tigers roar (or so it's said)
So does the monster under your bed.
I'd like to hear you roar a bit,
I really like the sound of it.
Fill the room with growls or cheers,
It'll drown out, perhaps, the roar in my ears.

Summer's End

There's nothing wrong with today,
It's perfect in every way.
The sun is placing my face
In a full-on, loving embrace.
There's only one thing that's a bummer,
It happens to be late summer.
So instead of happily sunning,
I'm thinking about what's coming.

A Quest for Questions

If you mull too hard, will you grow a mullet?
When seagulls eat, do they use their gullets?
Should I sit on a pillow when I swallow a pill?
If I choose the filet, will I eat my fill?
Shouldn't your butt have a button or two?
Doesn't your mutt ever mutter to you?
Do you think that your dollar bill is named Billy?
Do you think that a window sill is quite silly?
What's that you ask? When will this end?
When the questions all become natural, my friend.
In other words, you won't need me for suggestions,
You'll needle yourself with these ludicrous questions.

Solar Camels

I wish I were a camel
Whose humps could store the sun,
I'd sit outside in temperatures
That reached a hundred and one,
Soaking summer heatwaves
Til my eyeballs started to smolder.
I'd store up all those sun beams
Til my humps were two big boulders.
Then around about January
When it's cold and gloomy for days,
I'd open up my sun humps
And bask in those stored-up rays.

The Song of Autumn

Crunch go the leaves beneath my feet.
How did that sound become so sweet?
A sandpaper rhythm, a sidewalk scour,
Crunch is a sound that my ears devour.
I scruffle and fluffle and shuffle along,
Humming a crackling, leaf-loving song.
A swish-slide crickle, a slide-swish dance
While twigs and leaves hitch a ride on my pants.
That's the rhythm that has me enthralled,
The papery thin, sweet din of the fall.

Dinosaur Shopping Mall

Step up! Step up! Come one! Come all!
To the newest dinosaur shopping mall.
We built it big; we built it wide.
How else could we fit all those reptiles inside?
What will they buy? A new pair of flippers?
Triceratops high tops? Diplodocus slippers?
What will they eat? (Not each other, I hope.)
Pizza? Spaghetti? A licorice rope?
Here comes Iguanodon with Ankylosaurus,
Off to the bookstore to buy a thesaurus.
"Mom!" says a young one. "Buy me these, please!"
He points to a pair of red dinosaur skis.
"Will you use them?" asks Mother. "Yes, Mom, I will!
I'll use them to ski along Sauropod Hill!"
Here's Stegosaurus with plates and sharp spikes.
I wonder what movies this dinosaur likes.
Our mall has six theaters. There's plenty to see.
A movie called *Meteor!* And *Raptor Rage III*.
Oh, what a mall. There are so many stores.
Stores for plant-eaters and, yes, carnivores.
Sinosauropteryx wants a new dress.
She's eyeing a classic Triassic no less.
Parasaurolophus needs a new hat.
It's hard to find hats for a head shaped like that!

That's why he's here at the Dinosaur Mall.
We have what you need be you tiny or tall.
No matter what shape, there's a store here for you.
Yes, Pentaceratops shops with us too.
Look! Spinosaurus! Man, he's titanic.
It looks like our shoppers are starting to panic.
That's what it's like every day here, oh brother.
We have to keep shoppers from eating each other.
But we love it, it's true. Our jobs are the best.
Even though with these dinos we never can rest.
We're proud of our stores. It's the best place of all.
The newest dinosaur shopping mall.

Everything Should Have Pockets

Pants and skirts,
Blouses and shirts,
Everything should have pockets.

Hats and shoes,
Big hair-dos,
Everything should have pockets.

Cats and dogs,
Chickens and frogs,
Everything should have pockets.

Kangaroos
(They already do),
Everything should have pockets.

Busses and cars,
Electric guitars,
Everything should have pockets.

Rice and beans,
Kings and queens,
Everything should have pockets!

Plate and bowls,
Squirrels and moles,
Everything should have pockets!

A flute, a gong,
The end of this song,
Everything should have pockets!

Time to Choose

Cake or pie, cake or pie,
Which would you choose to eat and why?
Choosing cake? Big mistake.
Cake isn't food, it's a venomous snake.
Cake's a bruise, a baker's ruse,
A frivolous tidbit of tabloid news.
A primping Adonis, cake is dishonest,
It can't follow through on one pitiful promise.

Choose the pie! I'll tell you why:
Pie won't leave you. Pie doesn't lie.
Pie isn't callow. Pie isn't shallow.
Pie doesn't render your tastebuds fallow.
Pie is that space that you love to embrace,
A harbor you might call your happiest place.

Soon there might emerge a fight,
An epic war to judge who's right.
One warm July, an army guy
Will ask you, "Is it cake or pie?"
One will lose. You'll have to choose.
You won't be able to refuse.

That day is nigh, it's do or die.
By all that's holy: choose the pie.

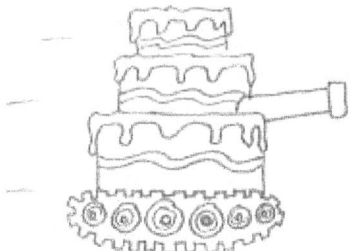 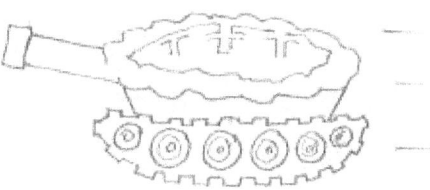

Friend Window

In between the world and me
Sits Friend Window.
"I'll show you all there is to see,"
Says Friend Window.
"The sky, a kite, a traffic light.
A bush, a tree, a whirring bee.
A cloud, a bug, a garden slug."
Thanks, Friend Window.

"Look it's Mrs. Ethelred,"
Says Friend Window.
"Watering her garden bed
Over by the willow.
There goes Pat, that sneaky cat,
Can you spy the dragonfly?
Oh, the sights! The city lights!"
Sighs Friend Window.

Sometimes what I see out there
With Friend Window
Isn't really truly there.
Right, Friend Window?
A squirrel in pants, a lizard dance,
A purple star, a robot car,
A fairy glade, a chef parade!
Fun Friend Window!

Where Did It Go My Tomato?

I thought I bit a tomato,
But where in the world did it go?
Not into my mouth
Or to my stomach down below.
It isn't on my dinner plate,
It's gone without a trace.
Oh, there it is, I see it now.
All over my dad's face.

Can You Top That?

At four years old I displayed a giant cartwheel across the floor.
"Can you top that?" asked my parents. "Maybe bigger, better, more?"
Then I performed a wheelie on my bike when I was eight.
"Can you top that?" said my friend. "I bet backwards would be great!"
At twelve I learned the vibraphone, guitar and ukulele.
"Can you top that?" asked my teachers. "Learn the harp and organ maybe?"
At seventeen I won eleven medals in gymnastics.
"Can you top that?" asked my coaches. "Fifty more would be fantastic."
And that is why, dear audience, I stand before you now,
Balancing on pinky toe atop this charging cow,
Juggling six axes, ten piranhas, and a plow,
Praying your reaction will be nothing less than "Wow!"

How Do You See the Mimliodee?

The Mimliodee has never been seen,
Is it red or yellow? Is it orange or green?
Maybe it's a blend of magenta and tan.
Scientists say it's as large as a van.
But scientists, sadly, don't always agree
Because some of them say it's as small as a bee.
Is it a mammal? A bug? A crustacean?
You'll just have to use your imagination.
In 2007 a bone was discovered,
By 43 layers of earth it was covered.
It didn't belong to a dinosaur, no,
A bird or a rhino or anything known.
One professor named Dr. O'Leary
Came up with a rather interesting theory:
"The bone doesn't fit a known category,
It therefore belongs to the Mimliodee."
They built a large lab to try to agree
On any one trait of the Mimliodee.
They filled up the lab with tools and computers,
Researchers, specialists, teachers and tutors.

Someone invented a Mimlio-scope,
Which might see the Mimliodee they all hoped,
But when it was looked through, they saw only dust.
They had to admit the whole thing was a bust.
Someday we'll know its exact shape and size,
The sound of its voice and the strength of its eyes.

We'll say for sure and once and for all
If it's round or square, if it's short or tall.
Some might cheer when they hear this news,
But I'll have a serious case of the blues.
Because whatever it looks like, whatever they find
Won't look as good as the one in my mind.

Isn't it perfect that each of us sees
A totally different, distinct and unique,
Singly original Mimliodee!

The Kid in the Bathroom Mirror

There's a kid in the bathroom mirror.
And something about her is not quite right.
She's mean and she's rude and she's impolite.
It's plain that she could never be
As saintly and well-behaved as me.

This kid in the bathroom mirror,
Someone should tell her that it's rude to stare.
And who still carries a teddy bear?
Don't stick your tongue out they say,
But she does it to me nearly every single day!

She must have been raised by wolves
Or a pack of feral cats.
How else would she have grown to be as mean and rude as that?

This kid in the bathroom mirror,
She should know not to be a copycat,
But everything I do, she does right back.
One day I caught her sneaking in
With an extra slice of pie that was clearly forbidden!

She must have been raised by wolves
or a pack of feral cats
How else would she have grown to be as mean and rude as that?

But the worst thing about her, the tragedy,
is yesterday she told me she thinks she's me . . .

More Homework

A pile of homework stood on my desk,
Two English essays and a history test.
I completed them both with minimal stress . . .
Then there was more homework to do.

I worked on that pile til six AM.
I finished next week's, and next month's and then
I caught myself up to semester's end . . .
Then there was more homework to do.

With marmalade jars and a TV screen
I constructed a trustworthy time machine.
I visited each of the homework years
Of my lower, middle and high school careers.
Gathering past and future selves,
We did all my homework, K through twelve.

Every assignment prompt and correct,
Neatly completed and quadruple-checked.
I graduated then with a 4.0
And knew all there was for a person to know . . .
Then there was more homework to do.

All of a sudden, fortuitously,
I received a bite from a magical flea.
Omnipotent powers exploded in me!
I abolished all homework immediately.
Not just the work but the concept as well;
The notion of homework itself was dispelled.
No one recalled it. It never existed.
In no dimension had it ever persisted.
And to make sure homework was permanently prevented,
I denied humankind the will to invent it.
It was never assigned nor ever had been
Nor would it ever be assigned again . . .

. . . then there was more homework to do.

Who Loves the Rain?

Gardening is good for the spirit,
Especially on days when it pours,
For you're stuck inside complaining
That you can't do a thing outdoors.
But then you think of your garden;
Most likely your plants love the spray.
And you smile despite the rain drops;

. . . at least someone's enjoying the day.

Semantic Antics

I organized my bedroom,
Which makes you think I cleaned it,
But really I just stored the mess
Where nobody will see it.

Pandas

Don't ask a panda for comfort
When feeling despondent or blue.
It might rub your shoulder consolingly,
Or give you a head pat or two.
While you're thinking, "This panda's amazing!
In a crisis it knows what to do!"
The panda keeps rubbing and patting,
Thinking, "What a sweet stalk of bamboo."

The End of the Book

When you get to the end of a book,
It's always worth taking a look
To see if there's anything more in the pages leftover.
Another poem perhaps?
Folded up treasure maps?
Or maybe somebody pressed a four-leaf clover.

Oh, the adventurous mind,
Always hoping to find
A secret goldmine buried beneath the rocks.
Or wondering what lies in
The land beyond the horizon,
Or which prizes hide in the pit of the cereal box.

And now here you stand
With a book in your hand,
And you've come to the collection's final stages.
What will be there?
Do you seriously dare?
All that remains is to turn the remaining pages . . .

About the Author

Adam Stockman is a school librarian in Westchester County, NY. He wrote his first poem in Second Grade entitled, "Making My Bed." Since then, he has written over a thousand poems. He also sings, plays guitar, and writes songs for kids in the band The Ossibles.

www.ingramcontent.com/pod-product-compliance
Lightning Source LLC
Chambersburg PA
CBHW071011160426
43193CB00012B/2006